Leadership

The Top 100 Best Ways To Be A Great Leader

By Ace McCloud
Copyright © 2014

Disclaimer

The information provided in this book is designed to provide helpful information on the subjects discussed. This book is not meant to be used, nor should it be used, to diagnose or treat any medical condition. For diagnosis or treatment of any medical problem, consult your own physician. The publisher and author are not responsible for any specific health or allergy needs that may require medical supervision and are not liable for any damages or negative consequences from any treatment, action, application or preparation, to any person reading or following the information in this book. Any references included are provided for informational purposes only. Readers should be aware that any websites or links listed in this book may change.

Table of Contents

Introduction 6

Chapter 1: Developing Your Leadership Skills 8

Chapter 2: The Top 100 Best Ways to Be a Great Leader
.... 10

Chapter 3: Building Leadership Skills.......................25

Chapter 4: Leadership Resources 30

Conclusion..33

My Other Books and Audio Books...........................34

DEDICATED TO THOSE WHO ARE PLAYING THE GAME OF LIFE TO **WIN** KEEP ON PUSHING AND NEVER GIVE UP!

Ace McCloud

Be sure to check out my website for all my Books and Audio books.

www.AcesEbooks.com

Introduction

I want to thank you and congratulate you for buying this book: "Leadership- The Top 100 Best Ways To Be A Great Leader."

Leadership is a very valuable life skill. A person who has excellent leadership skills is often more successful in both their work and personal lives. Your leadership skills can define the success of how you run your home, raise your family, influence others, and earn your salary among many other important things. You may have found yourself believing that people are born with great leadership skills. However, that's not necessarily true! Anybody can be a great leader! All it takes is the ability to learn and master the skills and knowledge behind great leadership!

Leaders are the ones who face challenges head on and never give up until a solution is reached. In a broad sense, people with great leadership skills have the ability to change the world. Think about President Madison, who was responsible for the Bill of Rights—the document which protects you from getting in trouble for speaking freely or being illegally searched by the police among other liberties. Without great leadership skills, he may have never made it to the White House and you could of been living in a very different world today. Martin Luther King, who fought for civil rights and the end of racial segregation, also had excellent leadership skills, as he influenced many people during his time. Though President Madison and Martin Luther King were both political figures, leadership is far more than political. Steve Jobs was a leader in technology and without his great leadership skills; you might not have an iPhone, iPad or similarly inspired device. Without Jonas Salk, a leader in science, you may not have had the protection you currently do against various viruses and illnesses. The examples of how great leadership affects the world are endless. Many great stories and books are filled with the legends and history of great leaders. Even more great leaders have existed throughout human history who you have never heard of, but they existed and were great nonetheless.

Leadership is important whether you are influencing the world or just a small group of individuals. People with great leadership skills often climb the ladders at their jobs quicker, are more respected, make more money, and are more memorable than other people. If you are a parent and your leadership skills are weak, you may not find that your children are not behaving as you'd like them to. Students who are leaders often have better education prospects and often carry their leadership skills into the real world. In short, there are virtually no negatives to strengthening your leadership skills—your life might be great right now and that's good—but the better you can get as a leader, the better off you can be. Once you have mastered your leadership skills, you will find yourself with the power and opportunities to open more doors for yourself and others than you've ever thought possible.

Most importantly, leaders affect other people. If you're a leader at your job, your actions can directly affect your teammates. If you're a leader as a parent, your actions can directly affect your children. If you're a leader at your school, your actions can directly affect other teachers and students. Great leaders produce winning results by encouraging the strength and good morale of their team. Great leaders inspire those around them to become great leaders themselves. Many people look to their leaders for advice and great leaders always try to point them in the right direction. All in all, people who are great leaders are always impacting the world, one way or another, whether on a national scale or just a local one.

The problem with leadership is that many people's leadership skills are just undeveloped or tainted with impure desires. Depending on how you were raised, the environment you work or have worked in, and the people who have come in and out of your life, your leadership skills may or may not be at their best. The key is to remember that no matter what, you are a leader, even if you don't know it yet! You can do great, positive things with your life while positively impacting the lives of others in the process. Leadership skills will benefit you all throughout your life. Many people simply don't even try to take advantage of their ability to be a leader.

You're already reading this book, so I can tell that you are interested in stepping up and bringing out the best in yourself and others. You've already made it through step one! Now it's time to change both your life and the lives of others for the better.

This book contains proven steps and strategies on how to take your leadership skills to the next level. Throughout the rest of this book, you will learn the top 100 best tips, tricks, and strategies for becoming a great leader. You will also learn how to integrate those skills into a daily action plan that you can use to continually get better and better. Finally, you will discover some great resources on leadership that you can use anytime you wish to stay motivated and inspired.

Chapter 1: Developing Your Leadership Skills

One of the greatest debates in the topic of leadership is whether great leaders are born or made. While some people swear that great leaders can only be a product of nature, others are convinced that anybody can transform into a leader despite their background, upbringing, etc. While there is currently no scientific evidence to prove either or, many people are split on the issue.

Here are my thoughts on whether people are born or made into leaders: leadership and management are two different things. While anybody can be a manager, leadership requires a positive attitude and outlook on life. I think that is where most people get confused. Anybody can say, "Okay, we need to get X,Y, and Z done. I'll give project X to employee A, project Y to employe B, and project Z to employee C and everything will run smoothly." What many managers don't take into account is that the people they lead are not robots—a manager must *lead* their team towards results by setting a good example. They can't just hand out orders and then hope that it all comes together by the end of the day. Those around them need to actually respect them before you can truly get great results. If those around you feel that you are only looking out for your own self-interests, then you are sure to get lackluster results and attempts on your leadership. While some may be gifted with natural talents that are conducive to great leadership, those talents will still have to be improved upon and others developed so that you can truly be respected as a leader. I'm sure you've come across many situations in life where selfish and unqualified people have been given leadership positions. I know I have and it is always very disappointing. Just because someone is in a leadership position it does not make them a qualified leader.

The Basics of Leadership Development

Self-confidence is one of the biggest foundations of becoming a good leader. The more confident you are, the better you can lead people. Have you ever heard the saying, "You can't love somebody else if you don't first love yourself?" It's kind of the same thing when it comes to leadership. If you can't trust your own instincts, how can you expect others to trust you? If you are insecure about your abilities, how can you be confident in the abilities of your people? If you can't handle failure, how can you help your employees when they come in contact with an obstacle?

Again, the good news is that anybody can go from having low self-confidence to having a high level of self-confidence. It will be different for everybody but it is possible. For much more information on how to boost your self-confidence so that you're ready to lead a team, check out my bestselling book: Self-Confidence.

Another foundation for becoming a good leader is to be in great health. Your health is what keeps you up and running at peak performance and it helps you get through the day productively, so if you're not in good health, it can be very hard to lead others. Leaders in particular often find themselves under mental stress due to the many responsibilities that they have. Leaders must also have good stamina, as they often travel, work alongside their team, and make important presentations. Maintaining your physical health as a leader is a vitally important. Eating a regular, balanced diet and working out are great ways to start. For more information on improving your health and energy, I invite you to read my two very popular books: Ultimate Health Secrets and Ultimate Energy.

Determination and persistence are crucial for becoming a great leader. Even if you are the type of person who may be more of a natural-born leader, it is still important to pursue and develop your skills. Leadership skills and qualities are like muscles—if you don't use them, you can lose them. Doing things such as breaking bad habits, staying encouraged even during times of peril, and overcoming fear and obstacles, among other factors, are all a part of staying determined and persistent towards your leadership goals. The better you can exert self-discipline, the better kind of leader you can be. For more detailed information on how to master these skills, be sure to check out my extremely popular book: Influence, Willpower, and Discipline.

Having good role models can also tremendously help you in becoming a better leader. When you have a successful person to admire, model yourself after, and look up to, you pose a much better chance at learning about leadership the right way. What's a better source of information than someone who has already been hugely successful in leading others? Your role model in leadership can be a boss, an older family member, a teacher, a celebrity, a famous CEO, or anybody else you admire who leads by setting a good example. In Chapter 2 we will go into further details for finding great leadership role models.

Finally, there are specific character traits that you can learn and develop that will ensure that you are leading people to the best of your abilities. In Chapter 2, you will learn about these in more detail. The important thing to note is that these character traits can make or break you as a leader. Remember, you can be a great leader! Anybody can become a leader as long as they incorporate a good strategy for increasing their skills and never give up. By developing your leadership potential, your life can become much more enjoyable. You can increase your earning potential, inspire others, and become very successful in life.

Now it's time to find out what it takes to become a great leader!

Chapter 2: The Top 100 Best Ways to Be a Great Leader

Planning Skills

Be a Planner. One great way to better manage your time and projects is to make a plan. As a leader, you probably know what you need to get done and who you'll be working with in a given day. Each morning, try to create a rough plan for the day in your head, on the computer, or on paper and then follow it. Without a good plan, you might find it easier to put off important tasks and waste a lot of precious time.

Assess Your Situation. If you're strapped for time, take five minutes to step back from your daily operation and do an assessment. See if there is anything you can identify that might be taking up more time than you originally planned for. (For example, if you're managing a restaurant, you might suddenly get hit with an unexpected rush that sets you back 20 minutes.) Try and create a contingency plan that can be used if things are not going according to the original plan. You can also consider eliminating strategies that are not working and implementing something new that may allow things run smoother.

Prioritize Tasks. When planning out your daily operations, prioritize your tasks. This way, if you do run into any unexpected obstacles, you can eliminate some of your less important tasks if needed. As a leader, your team will look to you to find out which tasks can be put off and which ones should be completed as soon as possible. This is vitally important, so as a good leader you need to know exactly what needs to get done for your team to be successful.

Keep a Schedule. As a leader, you will often have many daily responsibilities. If you're really busy or if you just have a bad memory, sometimes your daily tasks can become overwhelming. One great idea for becoming a successful leader is to keep a schedule, whether this a formal schedule that includes your teammates or just a small agenda book that is intended for your use only.

Set Goals for the Big Picture. As a leader, it is important to keep the big picture in mind when planning your organization. When planning goals, be sure to focus on both your long-term goal and your short-term goals. It's a good idea to set goals that are measurable and realistic; otherwise you may not get very far. Goal-setting in any organization is vitally important for staying on track. As a leader, your job is to know which goals to set. It is always a good idea to start a goal off with the phrase: "I will easily..." I also highly recommend the professional goal setting program called: Goals On Track. It is the best goal setting program that I have found on the market.

Think Proactively. Thinking proactively can help you stay a couple of steps ahead, thus reducing the chances that you will run into problems in the future that could have been avoided. Always try to be prepared for changes, surprises, and obstacles. Preparing yourself for potential future problems can help you stay calm in times of distress and help lead your team to success if these situations should arise.

Be Adaptable. As a leader, you will often be required to travel, meet new people, and be ready to tackle unfamiliar situations. When you're not willing to change or go into unfamiliar situations with positive thoughts and energy, you could hinder your success potential as a leader. Practice adaptability and build it up for whenever you find yourself in a new situation. Things are not always going to go your way. So instead of throwing a fit, try and be adaptable and make the best of any given situation

Character Skills

Be Honest At All Times. To be a leader in any situation, being honest at all times is crucial because you need to have the respect and trust of others. Your level of honesty and integrity is a reflection of yourself and how others will perceive you. It builds good character and makes you a trustworthy and respected person. Finally, if you present yourself as an honest person, your employees will likely model your behavior. In business and in life, your reputation is everything.

Practice Self-Motivation. As a leader, what motivates you? If there isn't a specific reason why you're leading a team, you may find it harder to be a good leader. Asking yourself why you're a leader can be very empowering. Are you doing it to support your family? Do you have a passion to teach others? Find your self-motivation and you will find it much easier and fulfilling to lead. If you need help with this, be sure to check out my book devoted solely to: Motivation.

Be Authentic. As a leader, your team will be looking to you for guidance. If you're authentic, you can better lead your team with consistency, communication, and encouragement. Authentic leaders have an easier time identifying the strengths in their team members, which is important when it comes to delegation. People who are led by authentic leaders often go on to succeed themselves because they believe and trust in their leadership.

Be a Good Communicator. When you're a leader, good communication is crucial. It's easy to let yourself know what you want others to do. However, unless you speak those thoughts clearly, your team will not know your expectations. Communication is important if you want to lead your team to success! Knowing how to communicate can help you work more intelligently toward a goal, train others easier, and foster an open and productive work environment.

Have a Sense of Humor. When you're a leader, you will likely run into some mishaps—perhaps your website crashes right before a big promotion or your latest business plan flies out the window of your car. When those things happen, it is important to approach the situation in a calm manner. Having a sense of humor and knowing how to laugh at your mistakes can help inspire your employees to not take failure so seriously. Research even shows that having a sense of humor can actually improve productivity. For some great tips on how to expand your sense of humor, please check out my book: <u>Laughter and Humor Therapy</u>.

Display Strong <u>Self-Confidence</u>. As much as you may wish that every day goes great, unfortunately, that is not the reality of the world. You will likely experience some days that just seem horrible and you may wonder what the hell is going on. In those cases, you must have a strong sense of <u>self-confidence</u> to stay a strong leader. As the leader, it is your job to stay strong and motivated despite any obstacles. It will also set a great example and inspire your team to become confident too—which can only help improve workplace happiness and productivity. No matter how terrible you may feel and no matter how dire the circumstances, be sure to put on a brave face and let the world know that you're still going to succeed. The ability to put on a good bluff or to just portray a solid sense of certainty that success is inevitable is a characteristic that many of the greatest leaders in history have possessed.

Be Committed. By staying committed to your work or your business, your employees will be more likely to stay with you in the long-run, despite any obstacles that come your way. Being committed to both your work and promises can help improve your level of respect among others, which can really boost productivity among your employees and others that you are leading.

Keep a Positive Attitude. When you're leading a team, having a positive attitude is another major key. Staying positive includes everything from not letting challenges discourage you to encouraging your teammates to stay positive. If your employees ever come to you with a problem, whether work-related or personal, always encourage them and give them the best advice possible.

Trust Your Intuition. When you are a leader, sometimes you have to lead your team into the dark, meaning that you might not know what to expect at all times. In that case, it is important to trust your intuition, especially when your employees come to you looking for answers. When you learn to trust yourself, it is much easier for your team to trust you.

Stay On Top Of Your Assumptions. By staying on top of your assumptions, you can lead your team ahead of the game. Challenging your assumptions can help you move from the status quo to exploring the ever-changing markets, which is important for not falling behind the competition.

Be Solutions-Driven. Great leaders know that sometimes they will face obstacles. They are prepared to come face to face with problems along the way. The difference is that successful leaders are solutions-driven—they focus on finding a solution rather than getting caught up on the problem.

Have a Flexible Perspective. Having a flexible perspective can help you open your mind to new leads and ideas. It can also help you stay ahead of the game by being able to see new connections and patterns in your market. Of course, you can still keep your old perspectives, but a great leader knows when it is time to switch things up.

Ask Questions. Asking questions of yourself and your team is important for staying active and ahead of the game. The key is to ask the right questions. Instead of asking questions about problems, ask questions about solutions. For example, instead of asking, "Why haven't we made any breakthroughs yet?" say, "What problems do our customers have and how can we solve them?" Asking the right questions can make you a great, innovative leader. Some of the greatest solutions and inventions in history have been made by people who have been able to find the answer to this sentence: "There has got to be a better way to..."

Lead Your Own Way. There are hundreds of books, courses, and teachings on leadership styles and management strategies. However, if you trust yourself and lead in a way in which you believe will succeed, you can bring your team ahead and you'll also become unpredictable—great for fighting off competition. Be sure to find out what your personal leadership strengths are and do your best to maximize them.

Be Organized. As a leader, it is essential to be organized. You should be on time to all meetings, have things ready when you promise, know where everything is, and help your team to be organized as well. If you are not organized and you're trying to lead a team, chances are your teammates will see that as an excuse to also not be organized. Being organized sets a great example and it can greatly help improve productivity.

Be Consistent. Being consistent is important as a leader because it can show your team that you are confident, organized, and committed to leading an operation. It can also help you build respect with your teammates. For example, if you trained your team on the correct way to complete an assignment and then you do the assignment sloppily, your leadership will be inconsistent and likely ineffective. The most respected leaders in the world are those people that can be counted on to perform at high levels consistently.

Be Passionate. When you are passionate in what you do, it generally tends to make you a more successful leader. That is because you are much more engaged and focused in your work. Most of your leading will come straight from your heart. However, this passion can be difficult to maintain months and years at a time. For more information on how you can discover what to do to remain inspired on a consistent basis, be sure to check out my book devoted solely to: Inspiration.

Embrace Change. As a leader, it is important to embrace change because you will likely see a lot of it. Your team members may change, your projects may change, or the direction of your business may change. The range of different changes is endless. It is important to not get too attached to the way things are, otherwise it will be harder to welcome change when it arrives. Always remember that change is often good!

Show Gratitude. Showing gratitude in life is a great skill to have, whether you are a leader or not. If you are a leader, it can be especially helpful. We live in a world where many people take things for granted, so if you go out of your way to thank others and show gratitude on a regular basis, you can become a very likeable leader. Thank your colleagues for opportunities and thank your team for all their hard work. You can never show enough thanks in your professional and personal life! One of the proven ways to improve your mood is to just silently in your head or out loud list all the different things in your life that you're grateful for.

Communication Skills

Be an Active Listener. Communicating with your team is important, but many people forget that listening is a type of communication. When you listen to your team, it helps them feel more important and valued. To actively listen, you can engage yourself in the conversation and focus on what's being said in the moment. You can nod and make other small gestures to ensure your speaker that you are listening to them. This is a critical skill that any great leader must have.

Practice Persuasion. Many great leaders are also great persuaders. When you're a leader, you have to be able to persuade others to believe in your cause, your image, and your reputation. Just trying to let it "play itself out" will most likely not get you much attention. You have to work at it and be passionate. For more information on being persuasive, check out my book: Influence, Willpower and Discipline.

Learn Negotiation Skills. When working with and leading others, sometimes it will be necessary to make compromises and work out deals. Most often, leaders negotiate with others about salaries, expenses and many other important matters. The key to being a good leader is to make a compromise that is fair and beneficial for both parties.

Practice Giving Clear Explanations. When you're leading others, it is important to provide your team with clear explanations. If your team is not clear on what you expect from them, it could cause a lot of problems down the road. Never leave your team in the dark and make sure that they know exactly what you expect of them and what their duties are.

Practice Speaking Professionally. When you speak clearly and grammatically correct, it makes you appear much more professional. It also helps people take you more seriously and understand you better. Use grammatically correct sentences and speak slowly and clearly. People will tend to find you more confident and much easier to look up to if you talk clearly and not too fast.

Practice Good Writing Skills. Many successful leaders have great writing abilities. As a leader, you will probably be communicating with your team via several channels. Professionally written emails, letters, and memos can attribute greatly to your leadership potential.

Develop Good Technical/Computer Skills. When leading a team today, it is important to understand and utilize modern technology. With the development of smart phone apps, powerful website platforms, and social media outlets, there are many ways to push your organization forward. While you may find it a good idea to hire somebody for the technological side of things, it is important to be aware of and up to date on technology.

Training Skills. Successful leaders are often also successful trainers. Teaching certain skills and specializations to your team can help boost morale, productivity, and relationships within the team. If you can create good training systems and utilize them efficiently, your success as a leader will be greatly increased.

Empathy. Being able to emphasize with others is an important leadership trait because it can help you to understand what other people are thinking and feeling. If people feel like you actually care about them, they are much more willing to work harder and protect you as their leader. Being empathetic can also help you to understand how your teammates react in different situations, which can help you in your planning. Being able to exert empathy can also help you to build valuable and important relationships in both your personal and professional life.

Use the Power of Touch. Slightly touching someone in an encouraging way, such as patting someone on the back or giving them a hand shake can make you a very likeable leader.

Talk to People About Themselves. When others are talking about themselves, it makes them like you so much more. Let's face it—who doesn't love talking about themselves? When you show that you're genuinely interested in another person, your chances for establishing a good relationship with them can dramatically increase.

Build Rapport. Rapport is an interpersonal communication skill that you can use to "hit it off" with others instantly. Building rapport means imitating another person's posture, making eye contact, asking personal questions (such as, how are your kids doing?), finding something in common (Oh you like swimming? Me too!), and being overall genuine. This can make you very likeable and successful in leadership.

Learn to Deal With Aggression. As a leader, you may come into contact with some customers or team members who are aggressive and hostile. This type of behavior includes swearing, threatening, emotional abuse, and racial or sexual harassment. When you are faced with an aggressive situation, there are several things you can do to deal with it. First, don't take it personally and just assume you're the one who happens to be the target. Using open, friendly body language, respecting the person's personal space and moving slowly can help. Listen to the person, show that you understand, and do your best to encourage the person to come to a positive solution.

Don't Use Too Much Jargon. Using too much jargon can often lead to communication barriers. When speaking to large audiences and your team, be sure to use words that are commonly understood by everybody. That way you, your team, and your audience can all be clear on the expectations.

Be Aware of Disabilities. If somebody on your team has a hearing disability seeing disability, or some other type of disability, be sure to remember that when communicating with your team. Being aware of the special needs of your team can help you optimize your communication and get more done.

Be Aware of Language/Cultural Differences. If you are leading a culturally diverse team, it is important to be aware of any language or cultural barriers that may exist. These barriers can often create confusion and embarrassment. If you are working with somebody from another culture, a good idea is to read up on their culture to learn how your culture differs from theirs.

Don't Stereotype or Make Assumptions. When working with others who range in diversity, it is important to forget stereotypes. If you have a person who may fit a certain profile on your team and you treat them differently, it could create drama, hurt feelings, or even a lawsuit, especially if the stereotype does not apply to them.

Keep Your Audience Engaged. When you are speaking to a large audience or giving a presentation, try to keep your audience engaged by changing the tone and pitch of your voice every so often. There is nothing worse than listening to a monotone voice for long periods of time!

Use Visual Aids in Presentations. When giving a presentation, be sure to break it up with visual aids such as charts, graphs, videos, and pictures. Of course, every slide shouldn't contain a visual aid or else you might overwhelm your audience.

Leave Time For Questions. Whenever you talk to an audience or your team, always leave extra time to answer questions. If you don't allow anyone to ask questions or if you rush through a presentation, it can make it look like you don't care and thus make you less respected as a leader.

Take Notes. Take notes whenever you can. Take notes when meeting with your team, learning new things, and during evaluations. Notes can help you retain more important information and you can always refer to them at any time.

Create a LinkedIn Profile. As a leader, creating a LinkedIn profile can be very effective. You can use LinkedIn to strengthen your leadership skills, chat with other leaders, and find leadership mentors. You can also connect with your team on there and collaborate that way as well.

Be Available. Depending on what kind of leader you are (for example, business owner verses retail store manager) it may be extra important for your team to know how to get in touch with you. If you're the type of leader who might do a lot of traveling, you should make yourself as available to your team as possible. You can exchange cell phone numbers, create a Skype account, or set up an email list so that your team members can easily contact you whenever they need you.

Personal Growth Skills

Write But Don't Send. When you're angry at an employee or teammate, the last thing that you want to do is to lose your temper. A good strategy for getting your negative thoughts toward somebody out is to write an angry email but don't send it—instead save it as a draft and then look at it when you've cooled off. Abraham Lincoln used to do this, except in letter format. This can save you embarrassment and words you wish you hadn't said in the future. Of course there were always be situations where anger is justified and you may need to take more serious actions. Just try and wait until you have had time to cool down and think the situation through totally before doing something rash.

Practice Decision-Making Skills. Decision-making in any situation can be difficult. Many people often find themselves in denial when they have to make a big decision and often do whatever it takes to put it off. Luckily, there are some great ways for decision-making to be easy and effective. See if you can downsize the decision into simple steps and analyze the consequences of all the different routes. If you have time, plan it out so that you have enough time to look at all of your options. Making a bad decision can oftentimes be better than making no decision at all. All great leaders have the ability to be decisive when needed.

Practice Good Ethics. As a leader, you will likely be working with people from different backgrounds and cultures. It is your job to ensure an ethical workplace environment that does not put any specific person in harm's way. Your priority should be to treat everyone fairly and equally.

Practice Good Time Management Skills. Good time management skills go hand-in-hand with productivity. The better you can manage your time, the more time you have to get things done. If your time management skills are not up to par, your productivity levels can go down. As a leader, it is important to practice excellent time management skills as well as to teach them to your teammates. For advanced information on being supremely productive be sure to check out my book: Ultimate Productivity.

Take Strolls. Taking a walk on your lunch break or in between your projects can help you get in some exercise and keep your physical health in good shape. Taking a walk on a nice day can also help you clear your mind and refocus your energy for when you go back to work.

Lift Weights. Lifting weights is a great type of exercise and if you have your own workspace, you can keep a small set of weights nearby at all times. If you want to boost your confidence, lifting weights is a great way to start. Lifting weights can help you become strong, thus boosting your self-confidence and making you feel great about yourself. People naturally like to look up to strong and healthy leaders.

Schedule in Cardio. Finding some extra time to schedule in cardio can be beneficial to you as a leader in a variety of ways. It can improve your blood flow, make you less likely to get sick, help to improve brain function, and it is also great for producing endorphins that will help you feel great. Regular exercise can also help many people sleep better at night. Cardio exercise pumps oxygen to your lungs and heart so you'll be able to boost your stamina, which is important for leading others.

Practice Yoga. Yoga is a great type of exercise for leaders because it is a very relaxing, calming activity. It helps stretch your muscles, clear your mind, and build strength. There are many different poses to try and many businesses offer yoga classes.

Take a Deep Breath Before Answering a Phone. As a leader, sometimes phone calls can be stressful. You might find yourself constantly answering a ringing phone or waiting for a very important phone call. Take a deep breath before answering the phone to help clear your mind and settle your nerves so that stress doesn't overcome you.

Use Your Hands to Talk. Moving your hands while you talk can help relay energy to your audience when you're speaking. It can also help you ease tension. Try bending your elbows slightly, resting your arms in your lap and letting your fingers come very close together.

Retreat To Your Secret Spot. Sometimes finding a nice, relaxing place in nature where you can enjoy the sounds of the birds among the trees or watch the sun rise and set can be a great escape from the stress of being a leader. Whenever you are feeling overwhelmed, see if you can spend a few minutes in a peaceful spot. Research shows that this can greatly reduce stress. If you can't physically go to your secret spot, it's always nice to have your own personal private getaway that you can imagine in your mind.

Apologize When You're Wrong. When you've made a mistake or said something to somebody and you know you were in the wrong, make it a point to genuinely apologize right away. Something as simple as saying you're sorry can be very effective. More often than not, the other person will be satisfied and you will be less stressed. It is tough to respect someone who will never admit when they're wrong.

Be Forgiving. If you are on the receiving end of an apology from a team member, don't forget to be forgiving. Holding grudges can be unhealthy both for personal health and workplace health, so unless you're dealing with something major, let the little things go. This is easier said than done, and being able to forgive can actually be one of the hardest things in the world or a person to do. But if you can master this skill, you will be much more effective as you will be able to focus on the present and future rather than constantly dwelling on traumas and anger from the past. For more help in learning how to forgive, be sure to check out my book devoted solely to: Forgiveness.

Keep Plants and Water Them. If your workspace allows it, keep some nice plants nearby and water them any time you're feeling stressed out. Research shows that watering plants can help you feel less stressed within 10 seconds. Plants also produce oxygen and are a good morale boost for the environment.

Try Aromatherapy. A great and easy way to reduce the stress of being a leader can be to try aromatherapy. When you're exposed to wonderful smells you can find yourself more relaxed and at peace. You can simply buy an oil diffuser and different scented oils to keep in your workspace. Some of my favorite scents are lavender and peppermint. For some great aromatherapy devices and essential oils, just Click Here.

Have Your Own Mentor. As a leader, you will probably serve as a mentor to somebody but what about yourself? You may be a leader, but leaders don't always have all the answers. Be sure to stick with somebody who mentored you when you were younger or have somebody who you can call on during difficult times to help guide you out of a tough situation. If you can't find someone in person, you can model yourself after one of your favorite leaders. My personal favorites have been Arnold Schwarzenegger and Tony Robbins.

Take Walks. If you are in a situation (a meeting or under a strict deadline) and you feel that your emotions are about to get the best of you, take a short 5 to 10 minute walk outside and let yourself calm down. Take deep breaths and wait until you can recompose yourself before going back in front of anybody. Then, focus on listening instead of responding. This can be very effective in staying on track for the day and not making strategic mistakes.

Embrace Humility. As I mentioned before, leaders don't always have the answers. As a successful leader, you must be willing to learn, work with others, and have new experiences. If you display arrogance, it can make you look insecure and unapproachable. You need to know who on your team is best suited for a task and be able to go to them for advice on that particular subject. Pretending that you know everything is not going to help you or your team be truly successful.

Find Your Flaws. Even if you strive to be a perfect leader, the truth is that nobody is 100% perfect. However, if you take the time to step back and critically analyze yourself (if you can't give yourself an honest appraisal, have a trusted colleague do it), you can become more in tune with your flaws. Then you can find ways to improve yourself in those areas or hire someone to compensate for areas you may be lacking in. For example, if you find that you often make promises that you can't keep, you can work on your accountability and on giving more accurate responses.

Create a Support Group. Even the best of leaders can find themselves caught up in feelings of discouragement sometimes. To stay on top of your game, create a support circle. It can include your family and friends or you can even meet up with other professionals. This can also help you stay on top of your collaborative efforts. Another name for a support group is a mastermind group in which you all work together to improve as a whole.

Be Resourceful. As a leader, you will probably have many people coming to you with questions. As I have mentioned before, it is true that leaders do not always have an answer. However, if you can go and find out an answer to a question, it can make you a much more effective leader. The key is to actually follow through on your promise, find out the answer, and deliver it. As a leader, it is very easy to find out answers, with the internet right at your hands. Just be sure the answers are accurate.

Stay Educated. As a leader, you will likely be responsible for leading a team through a changing market. For many businesses and organizations to stay successful, it is important to stay updated on current social and business trends. Staying educated is important for staying on top of your game. You can get educated on topics that you need to work on, such as marketing strategies or expanding your company, or on developing your personal skills so that you can function at peak performance.

Be Fearless. Many great leaders are not afraid to take risks. In fact, many leaders have become successful from taking risks. Don't be afraid to make mistakes, as mistakes are part of risk-taking and they can help you learn for next time. To learn more about how to conquer your fears, check out my book: Overcome Fear.

Take Pride in Appearance. As a leader, it is important to take pride in your appearance. It can help boost your self-confidence and it can inspire others to also take pride in their appearance. Dress well, clean, and crisp. Make sure your clothes are appropriate for your position. Keep your hair nice, make sure you smell good, etc. Practicing good appearance and hygiene can make a huge difference.

Smile. Smiling is key to being a great leader. Would you want to work under somebody who was never happy? Of course, you don't need to wear a smile 24/7 but smiling when communicating with team members, closing deals, or networking can really make a difference in whether you are an effective leader. Smiling is also an important part of building rapport.

Be a Coach. As a leader you are also a coach to your team. It is up to you to lead them, guide them, and educate them to ultimately get the maximum results. There is a certain art to coaching. As a coach, you should always be nonjudgmental about the person you're coaching. To ensure that you don't mistake coaching for mentoring, try to refrain from commenting and only answer open-ended questions. Never give out answers. Instead, let the person you are coaching explore and find them. The point of coaching is to be supportive of your team and to help bring out the best of their abilities.

Management Skills

Delegate Tasks. Having a solid ability to delegate tasks can make you an excellent leader because it can help you organize your business and it can help you build trust in your employees. When you've mastered the art of delegation, you can build a killer team—for example, you can hire somebody who is great at organization to handle emails and snail mail while you can hire somebody who is knowledgeable in social media to do your marketing, and so on. Together, you and your team can get twice as much done if everybody is working on something they're strong at.

Know Your Team Strengths. This is a subset of delegating tasks, but in order to delegate tasks effectively, it is important to know the strengths of your team. You wouldn't want to give tasks to somebody who is not strong in that area. Carefully review your team's strengths and delegate tasks based off that.

Encourage Creativity. There will be times in your leadership career where you cannot make a clear-cut decision. In those cases, you must be prepared to think outside the box, especially when your teammates are relying on you to lead them into a solution. Although it may seem tempting to take the easy way out, put your creative thinking hat on and think about your options before jumping to any decisions. Creativity can often help you to achieve incredible results. For more help on being creative, be sure to check out my book on: Creativity.

Be Inspirational. Having the ability to inspire your team is important for setting future goals, expanding your company, and running a successful operation. You can inspire your employees by complimenting them on their hard work or acknowledge the progress that they have made. For more information on how to become more inspirational, I invite you to check out one of my latest bestsellers: <u>Inspiration</u>.

Don't Settle on One Answer. When you were little, you were probably taught that there was only one right answer. However, as a leader, you must recognize that there can be several right answers. Even when you think you've found a good answer; remind yourself that there still might be a great answer. See if you can find multiple solutions.

Don't Settle on Solutions. Though time may be of the essence, it is important to explore all answers in-depth. Ask "what if" to your solutions in order to avoid future pitfalls. Make sure that your team agrees on a solution before it is implemented. Doing this can help you out greatly in the long-run.

Be a Mentor. When you're a leader, it is also important to act as a mentor. When you're a mentor to somebody under you, you help them avoid mistakes that you previously made and you can help point them in the right direction. When you're a mentor, it can make you very memorable and respected as a leader.

Teach Your Team to Embrace Failure. As a leader, you probably already know that failure can teach valuable lessons. However, your teammates may not understand that as well. Helping your team understand that failure can help them learn and become more powerful for next time can help you become a successful, respected leader. Help them find the most valuable lesson possible in whatever mistakes you or they may have made.

Be Available. As a leader, you are probably aware that time is one of your most valuable resources. However, many people work under leaders who refuse to give anybody a minute of their time. To be a successful leader, always make time for your team, even if you might not have it. This can show that you respect your teammates and their issues.

Genuinely Appreciate Your Team. What's worse than doing hours and hours of hard work and then having it go unrecognized? As a leader, it is important to help your teammates feel valued for all the time they have put into their work. Doing this can help you retain your best players and it can also inspire your team to work harder.

Tackle the Hardest Tasks Before Hiring Anybody. If you are able to master certain business tasks first, such as accounting or marketing, you can make better selections when it comes to hiring others. It also enables you to jump in on those tasks if extra help is ever needed.

Fight Negativity With Positivity. Negativity is inevitable. You will often run into negativity and it will always be there. You will always have people who like to focus on the negatives. In those situations, always try to bounce something positive off something negative because it can really lighten up the situation and take the pressure off. For example, if you have to deliver three projects within two hours, say something like, "Well at least it isn't 4 projects!" If you find that there is consistently one bad apple that is spoiling the bunch, then that is often a time for you to show some leadership skills by removing that person and replacing them with someone who is a more positive asset to the team.

Use Monetary Incentives Wisely. Money is a resource that motivates many people, but the key is to use it in a sense that will motivate people in the long-term. For instance, many salary raises only inspire a short-term motivation and then quickly become taken for granted. Bonuses are often a better option because they are one-time deals that your employees know can happen again with more hard work. For maximum results, make bonuses 10% of base pay.

Build Your Teammates. A great leader is always trying to build their teammates up and help them grow instead of leaving them where they are. The best way to help your employees grow is to hold them to a reasonably high standard but by being careful not to be too unrealistic. Push them to do their best and to go as far as you know they can without demoralizing them.

Foster Good Relationships. When there is a relationship between a leader and the team, there is more mutual trust and respect in the workplace. More trust and respect leads to more cooperation, which leads to higher levels of productivity.

Encourage Accountability. As a leader, it is your job to be accountable. In addition to yourself, make sure that you can count on your team. By ensuring that your teammates can deliver on their promises, you can increase your levels of productivity and run a smooth, productive work environment that has a good reputation.

Emphasize Importance on Team Work. As a leader, it is your job to place an emphasis on the importance of team work. Team work can help foster a productive, respectful working environment and can help keep your organization ahead of the game.

Get Feedback. The most important feedback that you can get is from the people who you are leading. Do not forget to communicate with your team as to your leadership style or what customers may be asking for. They can give you first-hand suggestions on what you're doing right and how you can improve. A good idea is to ask for feedback at least once per quarter.

Genuinely Care About Your Teammates. Genuinely caring about your teammates can help you become a great leader. While many leaders tend to focus on their business or company they work for, they often forget that it's the people who keep it thriving. Showing care for your teammates can also help improve the morale of the workplace. If your teammates believe that you are looking out for their best interests, they are far less likely to throw you under the bus if the opportunity presents itself.

Throw Celebrations. While you shouldn't make your work life one big party, it is important to share celebrations with your team. For example, if you've all put in double overtime on a project, kick back and unwind with a fun celebration. Celebrating big achievements can help avoid you and your teammates from burning yourselves out and are great for boosting the morale of your team. If you have a group of champions, they need to be rewarded properly.

Empower Your Teammates. Great leaders tend to empower their team rather than making them feel powerless and useless. Think of it this way—would you want to work under a leader who made you feel diminished? I can't tell you how many scumbag managers I had to work under when I was younger who ruled by threats and intimidation rather than adopting a truly respectable leadership position. These types of managers never lasted too long, and were often times taken down by the employees they mistreated.

Encourage Collaboration. Sometimes the best idea ever can stem from multiple minds. Great leaders encourage collaboration and appreciate feedback from all of their teammates. Encouraging your team to collaborate can also inspire them to work harder, as many people have passion for their own ideas.

Recognize the Benefits of Conflict. When conflict arises in the workplace, it is often seen as a negative thing. However, when managed correctly, conflict can be a good thing. Conflict can be an opportunity for people to communicate their feelings to each other and address the situation so that things can move along smoothly in the future.

Manage Conflict. As a leader, your teammates will often come to you when a conflict arises. The most effective way to manage conflict is to negotiate and come to a compromise or to have the two conflicting parties collaborate to a solution. Denying or avoiding the problem is not an effective way to manage conflict.

The Subconscious Mind. The power of the subconscious mind is truly immense. To truly reach your true potential, being able to program your subconscious mind correctly is of immense importance. The two programs that I personally use every day for this and highly recommend are Hypnosis Downloads and Subliminal Power.

Have Fun. Most importantly, don't forget to have fun. Being a leader can be a wonderful, exciting experience. While you should lead with a sense of seriousness, never forget to bring light to your leadership journey and to those who you are leading. Life is too short—don't forget to smile, laugh, and enjoy life while teaching others to do the same.

Chapter 3: Building Leadership Skills

Do you remember back in Chapter 1 when I mentioned that your leadership skills are like muscles—you have to use them or risk losing them? This chapter will go over some of the best things you can do at home to boost your daily leadership skills.

Reflect Daily and Create a Mission Statement. Reflecting on yourself each day is a great way to relax, get in touch with yourself and your personal mission, and to gain personal feedback. Ponder questions such as, "What do I stand for?" "Who am I?" "How do I want to influence other people?" Ask yourself these and other similar questions as a way to create a personal mission and vision. Once you've figured out what motivates you and why you want to impact others, write it down and work on it a little each day until you slowly start crafting yourself into the leader that you've visualized.

You can use this technique to be a leader in any area of life, not just at work. The good news is that leading at home often supplements your experience for leading people at work. Here is a good example of a personal mission statement that can be used for either your personal or work life:

I will learn how to balance my personal interests and my important responsibilities. I want others to see me as somebody to look up too, confide in, and trust. I will do that by respecting the privacy of others and by instilling confidence in the people around me. I will set goals for where I want to be at the beginning of every week and share them with my peers. I will be honest and do all my work with full integrity, even if it means admitting my mistakes. I will strive to improve every day and be the best leader I can possibly be.

Your mission statement can be as long as you want and you can change it anytime you feel the need, as it is completely yours. Reflect on this daily or at least once a week to ensure that you are leading others to the best of your abilities. Here are some more questions that you can ask yourself:

- Do I speak my truth?
- Am I leading people from my heart?
- Do I stand behind my values and morality?
- How courageous am I?
- How are my team-building abilities?
- Do I dream big enough?
- Do I care about myself in addition to my team?
- Do I focus more on perfection or doing the best job possible?
- Is what I am doing right now going to leave a legacy?

Reflect upon your passions—are you still passionate about what you've been doing for the last 5 years? If your answer is no, you might consider moving to a different industry. When you've lost your passion for something, your heart might not be into leading a team as strongly into as you could be.

Ask Yourself "Why?" Asking the question "why?" is a very powerful motivational technique that can help you get a jump-start on committing yourself to things. Remember, as a leader, you must keep your commitments, as many people will be relying on you. For example, if you have to figure out a way to boost your sales, you need to know why before you can truly tap your motivational potential. If you are truly motivated by leading your team to success as a mighty leader, then this can be your why. If you and your team will be eliminated from the company for lack of production, then you can use this to motivate you. You need to have a compelling reason as to why you will be accomplishing a particular goal to truly get the inspiration and motivation needed for success. For any goal that you make in life, whether it be personal or professional, be sure that you have a powerful enough "why" to motivate yourself and others to complete it. If you don't have it, sit down and brainstorm about it until you do.

Prepare For Rejection and Failure. As a leader, you will likely be rejected at some point or you may make a mistake. To many people, this can be a devastating and lead to discouragement and anger. However, strong and successful leaders must be able to navigate through the hard times and lead their teams to victory no matter what. A great exercise to strengthen your leadership skills is to prepare yourself for when you eventually come to any bumps in the road. In the next couple of sentences, you will read about some of the most common mistakes that leaders make—you may very well make the same mistakes as you venture on your leadership journey. However, having an idea of what to expect can allow you to handle the situation much more calmly once you're there.

Here are some common leadership mistake scenarios and solutions:

- One team member comes to you and expresses concern that you are not putting enough focus on giving the team feedback and being involved in the daily operations. One possible solution is to put aside extra time in your schedule for a meeting every so often with your team members individually. Another solution could be to change your management style—for example, if you normally worked in your office all day, try managing your team by walking around and be more hands-on.

- You assigned a team member with an important project but somewhere in the midst of the project, the specifications got misinterpreted. Your team member delivers the project, but it does not conform to the rules and demands of the receiving client. Now you've reached the deadline and you're forced to deal with an incomplete project. When a situation like that happens, you could review your communication skills and ask your team for feedback on how clear and involved you were. You can also make it a point to schedule "check-ins" with your team member to ensure that they are doing projects correctly.

- You and another team member become very close and soon the lines between "boss" and "friend" become blurry. Then you find yourself in a situation in which this team member begins to take advantage of you because they know you are more likely to go easy. This can totally trample your authority and influence over your whole team. While it is important to get along with and be friendly to your team, you should always keep an eye on your barriers. In a situation like this, a good idea is to prepare yourself to be direct with the person. Remind them of your professional relationship and the importance of treating every team member equally. Be firm and get the point across but do not go as far as to create bad blood or drama.

- Two team members are in conflict with each other. How would you handle the situation? Would you encourage them to collaborate? How would you reach a solution that would make everyone happy?

Eliminate Excuses. As a leader, your responsibility is to set a great example for your team. If you are a person who makes too many excuses, you may regret not taking responsibility for something later on. Making excuses may seem easy, but they are usually never a good thing. Do you find yourself making too many excuses? Excuses usually stem from fear and the good news is there are many ways to overcome fear and tackle your excuses head on.

For this exercise, take a moment and think about a potential excuse that you might let overpower you. For example, your excuse might be, "I could start coming down on the rules so that my team stops taking shortcuts but I am afraid they will not like me." Next, write down the positive things that could happen from carrying out that action. In this case, your team could become much more productive.

The next step is to turn your excuse into an inspiration. On a piece of paper or out loud, reword your goal. In this case, it could be something like, "I will start working with my team to stop taking shortcuts and to do things the right way. I will use my great communication skills to make it clear that I am doing the best for all of us." Now, don't you feel much more inspired to eliminate your excuses and take action?

Read Everyday. Reading is a great way to keep yourself updated on what is going on in the world and it is a habit that many successful leaders possess. Reading keeps your brain sharp and can help you learn things that you did not already know. There is always something new to learn, even if you already think you're an expert. The greatest geniuses in the world know that only a fool thinks that they know it all.

One great way to get into the habit of reading every day is to have a nice collection of self-development books or websites to go to. Books are also a great way to learn new things and I already know that you're a reader because you're reading this book right now. Even if you just read a chapter of something a day, you can continue to improve your mental sharpness, your ideas, and your intelligence.

Practice in the Mirror. Practicing in the mirror is a great way to practice improving your leadership skills. Have you ever heard that the way you perceive others is a reflection of yourself? Do you often find yourself losing your patience and having a short temper with others? If so, it may not be them—it could actually be you. Something that makes you angry about others might actually be something that is causing underlying anger in yourself.

By looking inside of yourself, you can usually find solutions to many of your problems. Literally looking in the mirror is also a great way to improve your leadership skills. You can practice making eye contact with yourself and you can practice public speaking. You can also pick up on distracting habits that you may have, such as swaying or fumbling your hands, and you can also work on mastering certain facial expressions that will come in extremely handy as a leader.

Practice in Front of a Wall. Practicing in front of a wall is what you can try after practicing in front of a mirror. The purpose of using a mirror is to analyze yourself and see what you can improve upon in terms of eye contact and distracting movements. However, to truly focus on your words, especially if you plan on making a speech or a big announcement, practice it in front of a wall. This way, you won't be distracted with visual cues.

Practice With a Pet. If you're extra nervous about giving a speech or facing a large audience, practice in front of a pet if you have one. Pets are nonjudgmental but are still living creatures, so practicing in front of one may give you some comfort and relief while preparing you for being in front of a large audience.

Surf the App Store. One of the top 100 ways to become a successful leader is to keep up on new computer applications and technology. With the abundance of smart phones, new computer software, and even smart TV's, it is important to keep up with the times. If you have some free time during the day, take a look on your phone or computer's app store to see if there are any new programs that you can download to help improve your or your team's organization and productivity.

Most app stores have downloads that can help you improve collaboration, team-building, communication, and more. There are even apps that you can download to have important alerts or motivating quotes delivered straight to your device.

New and useful business apps are being developed every day and as a leader, it is your job to find the best ways for your team to work together. Taking a look on the app store may become a habit that can benefit you and your team greatly.

Set New Goals Each Week. Goal-setting is an important part of being a good leader because as a leader, it is your job to get your team from point A to point B. Many leaders ultimately have their sights set on long-term goals, but often times, short-term goals can help you eventually reach long-term goals. Write down your top three long-term goals as a leader and figure out how you can break them down into short-term goals to reach them.

For example, if you're leading a fast food restaurant and you ultimately want your sales to increase by $3,000 a week, you could work toward that goal by retraining your staff on delivering top notch customer service and making sure that all of the food is quickly made, fresh and properly prepared. Making those small changes can help attract and retain more customers, therefore ultimately boosting your sales.

For the most advanced way of easily making and tracking short and long term goals, I highly recommend the program: Goals On Track.

Daily Action Plan For Improving Leadership Skills

As a leader, you can practice skills every day to stay successful and on top of your game. Having a routine is a great way to build a solid foundation for success.

-Set a designated bed time and wake up time and stick with them.
-Leave some extra time each day to do a quick workout.
-Eat a healthy breakfast for a powerful energy boost.
-Review your daily agenda and short-term goals for the week.
-Practice at least 3 strategies to improve leadership skills within your workplace.
-Compliment your team on their achievements and review what they could have done better.
-Use your free time to practice speaking in front of mirror, reading, keeping up on the latest technology, reflecting, or thinking creatively.
-Unwind at home and congratulate yourself for doing a great job and continuing to improve.
-Think and plan for future goals

Chapter 4: Leadership Resources

As we come to this final chapter, I hope you were able to learn everything you've ever wanted to know about leadership. Since many people learn differently, I have included a section where you can watch some great YouTube videos on leadership, all of which are some of my favorite videos. I have also included some of the greatest quotes on leadership by some of the most successful people in the world. I hope the quotes and videos are able to inspire you as they have inspired me.

Leadership Video Library

Lead Simply by Give More Media

How to be an Effective Leader by Scott and Camber

The Speech That Made Obama President by THNKR

Anthony Robbins-Becoming The Leader by Addicted2SuccessTV

Leaders Vs. Followers by LoveHealthWealthLaugh

The Difference Between Leadership and Management by Radicals4J

7 Essential Qualities of All Great Leaders by Brian Tracy

Six Secrets To Success posted by Travis Fisher

Famous Leadership Quotes

"Whatever you are, be a good one." - Abraham Lincoln

"Earn your leadership every day." - Micheal Jordan

"There are three essentials to leadership: humility, clarity, and courage." - Fuchan Yuan

"A leader is best when people barely know he exists, when his work is done, his aim fulfilled, they will say: we did it ourselves." - Lao Tzu

"A cowardly leader is the most dangerous of men." - Stephen King

"Leadership is lifting a person's vision to high sights, the raising of a person's performance to a higher standard, the building of a personality beyond its normal limitations." - Peter Drucker

"You manage things. You lead people." - Admiral Grace Murray Hooper

"Become the kind of leader that people would follow voluntarily; even if you had no title or position." - Brian Tracey

"Before you are a leader, success is all about growing yourself. When you become a leader, success is all about growing others." - Jack Welch

"I must follow the people. Am I not their leader?" - Benjamin Disraeli

"Effective leadership is not about making speeches or being liked; leadership is defined by results not attributes." - Peter Drucker

"Lead me, follow me, or get out of my way." - George Patton

"The first responsibility of a leader is to define reality. The last is to say thank you. In between, the leader is a servant." - Max DePree

"Leadership is influence." - John Maxwell

"People buy into the leader before they buy into the vision." - John Maxwell

"Outstanding leaders go out of their way to boost the self-esteem of their personnel. If people believe in themselves, it's amazing what they can accomplish." - Sam Walton

"Leaders think and talk about the solutions. Followers think and talk about the problems." - Brian Tracey

"Education is the mother of leadership." - Wendell Willkie

"No man will make a great leader who wants to do it all himself, or get all the credit for doing it." - Andrew Carnegie

"If your actions inspire others to dream more, learn more, do more and become more, you are a leader." - John Quincy Adams

"Leadership is unlocking people's potential to become better." - Bill Bradley

"Never give an order that can't be obeyed." - Douglas MacArthur

"Leadership and learning are indispensable to each other." - John F. Kennedy

"No man is good enough to govern another man without that other's consent." - Abraham Lincoln

"Leadership is the key to 99 percent of all successful efforts." - Erskine Bowles

"The final test of a leader is that he leaves behind him in other men, the conviction and the will to carry on." - Walter Lippman

Conclusion

I hope this book was able to help you to identify the skills and abilities that you can work on and utilize to become an admired and great leader.

The next step is to start implementing everything you have recently discovered into your life. Start small and pick a few things that you want to improve upon. Take the time to make a strategy that you can utilize to guide you to where you want to go. Remember, that as long as you never give up, you're bound to succeed. Build up a reputation as someone that can be trusted and counted upon, and those who follow you will emulate your good example. Take the time to make a clear vision for your goals and then strategize the best plan of action for getting there. Then follow your plan and lead others along with you towards victory! I wish you nothing but success in your journey through life and I hope that you will be a mighty inspiration to all those around.

Finally, if you discovered at least one thing that has helped you or that you think would be beneficial to someone else, be sure to take a few seconds to easily post a quick positive review. As an author, your positive feedback is desperately needed. Your highly valuable five star reviews are like a river of golden joy flowing through a sunny forest of mighty trees and beautiful flowers! *To do your good deed in making the world a better place by helping others with your valuable insight, just leave a nice review.*

Thanks and Best of Luck

My Other Books and Audio Books
www.AcesEbooks.com

Business & Finance Books

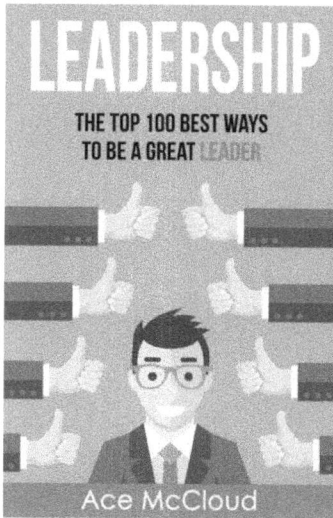

LEADERSHIP

THE TOP 100 BEST WAYS
TO BE A GREAT LEADER

Ace McCloud

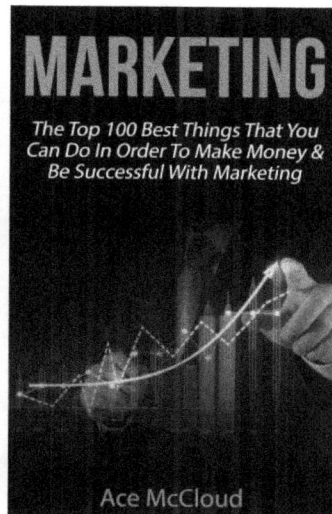

MARKETING

The Top 100 Best Things That You
Can Do In Order To Make Money &
Be Successful With Marketing

Ace McCloud

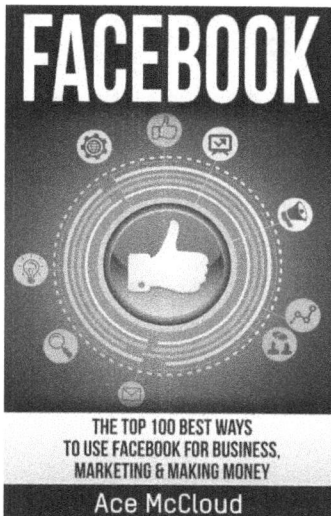

FACEBOOK

THE TOP 100 BEST WAYS
TO USE FACEBOOK FOR BUSINESS,
MARKETING & MAKING MONEY

Ace McCloud

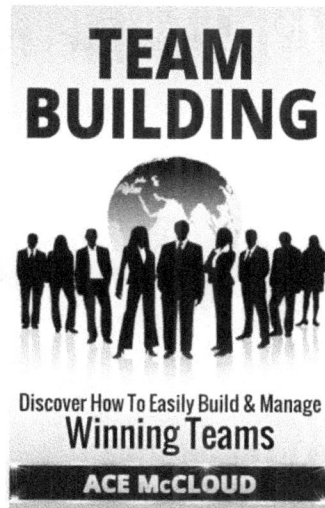

TEAM BUILDING

Discover How To Easily Build & Manage
Winning Teams

ACE McCLOUD

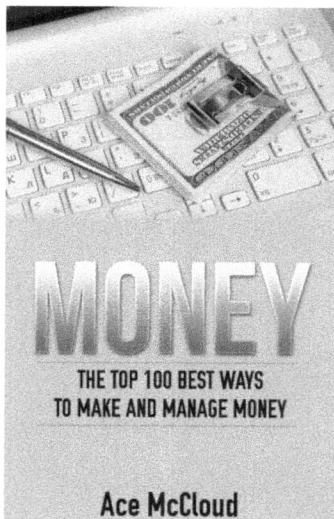

MONEY

THE TOP 100 BEST WAYS
TO MAKE AND MANAGE MONEY

Ace McCloud

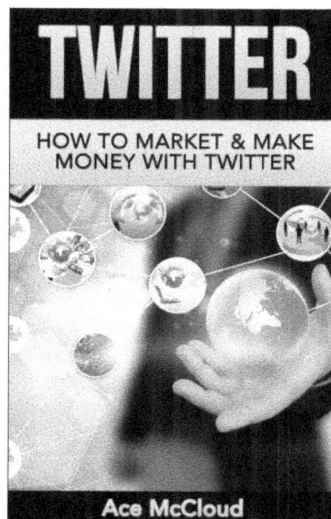

TWITTER

HOW TO MARKET & MAKE
MONEY WITH TWITTER

Ace McCloud

COMMUNICATION SKILLS

Discover The Best Ways To Communicate, Be Charismatic, Use Body Language, Persuade & Be A Great Conversationalist

Ace McCloud

YouTube

THE TOP 100 BEST WAYS TO MARKET & MAKE MONEY WITH YOUTUBE

Ace McCloud

Peak Performance Books

SUCCESS

SUCCESS STRATEGIES

THE TOP 100 BEST WAYS TO BE SUCCESSFUL

Ace McCloud

Ace McCloud

HABIT

The Top 100 Best Habits
How To Make A Positive Habit Permanent
And How To Break Bad Habits

MOTIVATION

MASTER THE POWER OF MOTIVATION
TO PROPEL YOURSELF TO SUCCESS

Ace McCloud

ATTITUDE

Discover The True Power Of
A Positive Attitude

Ace McCloud

SELF DISCIPLINE

Unleash The Power Of Self Discipline,
Influence And Willpower In Your Life
To Achieve Anything

Ace McCloud

Competitive Strategies

WINNING STRATEGIES

The Top 100 Best Strategies
For Peak Performance During Competitions

Ace McCloud

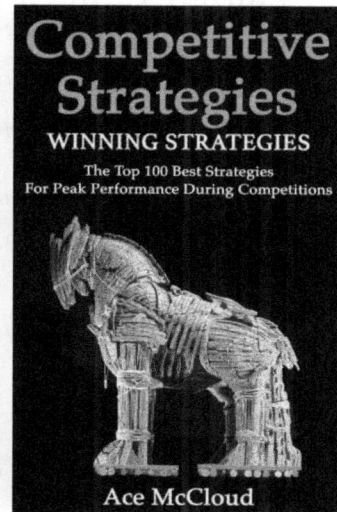

Be sure to check out my audio books as well!

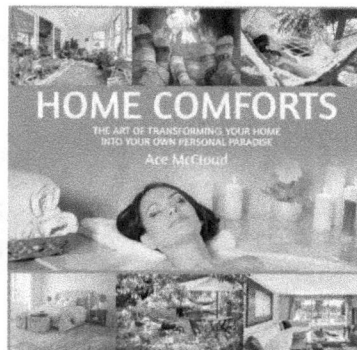

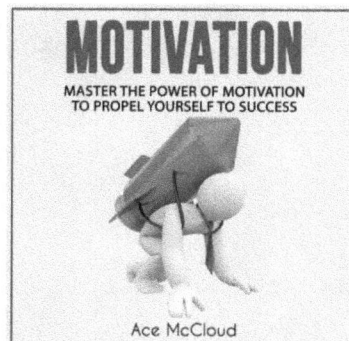

Happiness

The Top 100 Best Ways
To Feel Good & Be Happy

Ace McCloud

HOME COMFORTS

THE ART OF TRANSFORMING YOUR HOME
INTO YOUR OWN PERSONAL PARADISE

Ace McCloud

MOTIVATION

MASTER THE POWER OF MOTIVATION
TO PROPEL YOURSELF TO SUCCESS

Ace McCloud

Check out my website at: **www.AcesEbooks.com** for a complete list of all of my books and high quality audio books. I enjoy bringing you the best knowledge in the world and wish you the best in using this information to make your journey through life better and more enjoyable! **Best of luck to you!**

www.ingramcontent.com/pod-product-compliance
Lightning Source LLC
Chambersburg PA
CBHW081555220326
41598CB00036B/6680